IN THE HOUSE OF
LE PATRIARCHE

Peter Quiet

Translated by Paula Ferreira

Title
In the House of Le Patriarche

Author
Peter Quiet

Editor
Self-publishing

Publisher
Createspace/Peter Quiet
+351966629225
quito.arantes@outlook.pt

Translation
Paula Ferreira

Cover
Peter Quiet

Cover Photography
Paula Ferreira

Design
Createspace / Peter Quiet

ISBN: **978-1511408493**

The moral right of the author has been asserted

In memory of all my friends that perished victims of drug abuse, and all of the victorious who live today without drugs.

"Si vous osez entrer dans ce bâtiment, vous ne pourrez jamais le quitter".

Ricardo was about to catch the bus from Coimbra to Narbonne. His mother was by his side. She had always been helpful in his misfortune. She was his lifeline.

He was aware that he was going to a new world, unknown to him, in a certain way, although he had briefly visited the rehabilitation centre in Coimbra.

The year was 1990 and Ricardo would be thirty in a few months. The end of that winter was tragic to him, having been so close to death. He just wanted to get as far away as possible from his country, Portugal, where he had not found the best care for his health state. The social services had done a lousy work, which led him to two months in a hospital bed. All because they ignored the conditions in which he was institutionalized. He wanted to forget all those episodes he had been through, so he headed to France, almost as a family obligation. Fortunately, he was clean, without any sequels, which was not very common. He was conscious that he was relocating all alone to the centre in Narbonne. Usually, by indication of the centres, the residents should arrive with a family member, but it did not happen. He said goodbye to his mother and, from inside the bus, which was already running, he nodded through the window to her, in an emotionless farewell. It would be a very long journey that would enable him to reflect about his life. A new world was waiting, although he had been abroad before. This trip would take him directly to the rehabilitation centre. Physically, he was fit, but psychologically, he was not the same. Negative thoughts still lingered in his mind. He was not confident enough, yet. Probably, if he had returned home, things would turn back to worse again. So, his mother decided it was better, by precaution, to send him directly from Coimbra to France. The association had a rule that stated that the residents could not be from the country of origin of the centre. So, the Portuguese went to Spain or France and vice-versa.

The trip went well. When he arrived in Narbonne, it was hot, although it was still winter. It was usual to be bathed by the wind of "Suão", a southern gentle breeze that came from the north of Africa, as it was a Mediterranean city. Dropped by a motorway exit, he immediately called a taxi to take him to the community.

Ricardo knew that a new world was expecting him, a world that he still had not faced. Even though he had obtained information about the community, back in Portugal, it would be a new experience. Having arrived at the rehabilitation centre, he was greeted by a young woman who talked in Portuguese, and welcomed him. Paula, a Portuguese woman that had already been there for a year, left him apprehensive with her first question:

- Are you a negative?
- Excuse me?
- If you are not infected with HIV?
- Oh! No, I don't have the virus…
- Your name is Ricardo, isn't it?
- Yes... Pleased to meet you.
- You know, commonly there are two types of residents. The negatives, without the virus, and the positives,

that contracted the virus. That's it. We all live together with no problems. Are you clean or still suffer from withdrawal?

- I'm clean for two months now and I came by myself from Portugal, by bus.

Paula smiled and said:

- Weird, usually nobody comes clean, and never alone. They always arrive with family.

- I came of free will. I think it'll be good for me.

- I'm glad you think so. Now you'll be followed for two weeks by two residents that will give all the support you need.

The centre was all in baroque style, well preserved. It had a large patio with a garden. Ricardo began to know the residents, who were from several nationalities, mostly Spanish and Italians. The man in charge of the centre was a Spaniard named José, positive, of small talks, but nice.

They started to assign tasks after he became acquainted with the group. Ricardo and two others were assigned to the animals. On the other side of the road that passed by, there was a big field, belonging to the centre, where the football ground and the animals were located. Ducks, chickens, pigs, etc.

All the residents liked to take care of the animals, for the work was not hard and they felt more at ease, out of the sight of the centre supervisors. They just fed the animals and smoked some cigarettes.

That week, his companions were two Italians. Joseph was from Genoa and Pietro from Naples. Both were HIV-positive, but did not have any signs of the illness. Initially, Ricardo had some difficulty understanding them, even though they spoke Spanish, the official language of the centre.   Most of the organization was controlled by Spaniards. They were the majority.

He had to drink three times a day, for a week, the "Tisana", an herbal infusion that was supposed to remove toxins from the body. It tasted bitter, but there was no alternative.

There were still remnants of a snowfall from a week ago. It was February and it also snowed, although he was in the Mediterranean. Ricardo was trying to get to know the rules of the centre. He realised that the best posture he could have was not breaking them.

There were couples at the centre. They were few, two at least. The unions had rules. When they wanted to get together, they were sent to separate centres for two months. Pending on their behaviour, the supervisors decided if they were allowed. After that period, an approval was given and the union ritual was performed.

Ricardo would be present in a "mariage", in a few days. The "sevrages", or rookies like Ricardo were protected and, sometimes, had some privileges during a week. They were always the first to be served at meals, given extra candies, etc.

He felt good in the first days. Everything seemed simple to follow. Every day at 9 a.m. a group meeting was held, where everyone was asked to share their feelings and tasks were assigned for the day. After dinner, another group meeting took place, when the "sevrages" were invited to talk about their day. Ricardo always avoided speaking as he did not feel free to expose himself to the other residents.

He felt displeased about the food, particularly because it was past the expiration date. Usually, it was offered by supermarkets and distributed to the centres all over France. This made Ricardo feel insecure. One thing for sure, all of the food was analyzed to verify if it was suitable for human consumption. It was stored in large cooling chambers and sorted every day. The only thing that was bought, daily, was the bread, and it had to be consumed. There could be no spoiling.

Ricardo woke up, on his third day at the community, with the feeling that he would not see his family anytime soon. They had been his companions through past adversity in dark worlds, often tragic.

Everyone was there to recover for a new life. In fact, some of them were there to avoid being imprisoned by the court. It was given an opportunity to many that fell in the criminal world, due to drugs consumption, to rehabilitate themselves at the centre. It was better than being behind the bars, anyway. It was not the case of Ricardo. Fortunately, he did not go that far. He looked at his companions the same way, without discrimination. Everyone deserves a second chance in life to show that they want to be a part of society again.

A wedding was happening that day, by nightfall, at the centre. It was getting dark and, for his amazement, he started to see some colleagues coming by the patio, dressed in brown tunics. One of them carried a wooden cross, some two meters high, followed by his disciples, also wearing brown tunics. Next, the bride and groom appeared. She was an Italian from another centre. The groom was also an Italian, who was in charge of the centres of his country. Their voices sang some chants that Ricardo could not understand. He was stunned by the event. Meanwhile, others went to the bride and groom chamber and left it in a mess, leaving a goat from the farm inside. Actually, it was a common practice at that association. Going back to the ritual, at the moment of the blessing by the supposed priest, a window in the upper floor was opened and a bucket of animal droppings was dumped over their heads. Thus was the baptism/wedding of the new couple in the centre. Ricardo could not believe what had just happened. The bride and groom completely foul, ran away to their room, but they still had to face the goat and all the mess.

The residents were all euphoric, even without drinking any alcohol. It was not very often that they could witness such an original event. The Italians were the funniest ones and always ready to party.

Ricardo was on the verge of joining the group, after the week of "sevrage". Then, the privileges would be over and he would be like any other member. Once in a while, he missed his family very deeply. He was so far away and little could he do to minimize that anxiety. He could only take phone calls after that ritual week. The big thing was that someone from the centre was always listening to every phone call conversations from the residents. That made him confused and he felt some latent lack of freedom.

The week of "sevrage" ended and he joined the group. The daily tasks continued. A certain day, Paulo, a Portuguese who had already been at the association for three years, came to tell him that they would be spending two days together gathering food. Paulo was a lorry driver carrying cargo and food. Then, Ricardo felt happy for he was leaving the centre for the first time.

Paulo was an elegant man, tall, with dark skin and brown hair falling down to his shoulders. Ricardo felt empathy for him. They were able to eat fresh oysters with lemon juice, on the side of the road in their travels along the Mediterranean coast. It was the first time Ricardo ate oysters. They tasted a little bitter, but he could not avoid eating since he felt he would be disappointing Paulo.

The sun was hot. Spring had begun. The wind of "Suão", coming from the north of Africa, hit their faces with gusts of warm air. They would be staying at the reception centre in the city of Narbonne, that day. It was a small flat, but well arranged. Three residents were living there, who were replaced by others every six months.

Ricardo thought that if life at the association was always like that, it was not bad. However, reality was different and, after two days, he returned to the centre and back to the same routine.

There were many bushes to be planted and Ricardo volunteered to do it. All the entrance to the centre and adjoining buildings were embellished with cedars planted by him. José, who was in charge of the centre, did not question his work. He knew that Ricardo was peaceful and did not sneak around.

Sometimes he was mobilised to the animals. One time, he and three other colleagues, were given the task of killing about fifty ducks. After dead and plucked, the ducks were blanched in a two hundred and fifty litre steel barrel containing boiling water, to remove the remains of the feathers and its calamus, the part of the shafts closest to the body. The feathers were stored in bags to be sold later to pillow factories. The hardest part for him was the bloody way the ducks were sacrificed. But it had to be that way. They would provide food for several days. That same day, he went to the kitchen, to open the ducks, clean and pack them to later be stored in the freezers. He never thought that one day he could handle such a task. Far from the warmth of his parents, life led him to it.

Days were passing by. Sometimes, they got together to play football. And then he showed his talent, as a sublime forward being called Victor Paneira, Rui Barros or Futre. He used to play with the Spanish team against the Italians, who lost most of the time. Those were enjoyable moments and a physical exercise opportunity.

Two months had passed since he left Portugal. In a meeting, the chairman said that the Irish centre in Cork were in need of people that could speak English. He volunteered to go. He was the only one at the Narbonne centre that knew the language, so his community services had been promptly accepted.

He would make the trip to Paris with a lorry driver from the association, Pietro, an Italian, and later to the hangar at Chartres.

It was a long trip. The lorry did not go faster than thirty miles per hour but, actually, it was a funny adventure. They caught all kinds of weather, from heat to snow, on their way to the "City of Light". Pietro, of small talks, was concentrated on the road. Ricardo felt himself heading towards a different reality. It was a new destination, a new life experience.

When they arrived at the apartment in Paris, they went straight to bed. They were tired from the trip, the long hours on the road, riding at snail's pace. The following day they had to proceed to Chartres, where Ricardo would wait to be called to Ireland.

The lorry that Pietro was driving carried frozen goods and, at least, the freezing unit did not broke down. Pietro did not speak much. He was an HIV-positive that did not know how to face the illness. But still it was there, in his athletic body.

Finally, they arrived to Chartres. It was a world apart from the centre in Narbonne. Ricardo observed all the hectic movement of the residents. Big hangars stored all kind of materials. There were about one hundred and fifty persons. There were six other residents awaiting the call to Ireland, like Ricardo: two Italians, two other Portuguese, a Norwegian and a Spaniard. This was the group that would board the ferryboat to cross the English Channel.

The car with their luggage was already on board. Ricardo and his group walked towards the check-in. The customs officer looked at them with suspicion. So many nationalities in a small group, with such happiness in their faces, were very strange, indeed. All checked out ok, passports and identity cards were in order. So, they went aboard the big ferry that would take them to Irish lands.

The association, where Ricardo was redeeming from past mistakes, did not allow any alcohol. Its founder considered it just another drug, although legal, that led to relapses in other drug abuse, recurrently. Tobacco was allowed, but not the medicines used for psychiatric treatment. There was a latent concept that everything could be solved in a natural way, without the use of chemicals. That was a pertinent issue. The scientific community did not agree with the methods used in certain cases. Moreover, there was a slight disagreement between the French government and the association about certain requisites imposed by the supervisors of the centres. Indeed, there were residents that evaded the centres due to psychological incompatibility with the methods used.

Ricardo had never travelled in a ship of those dimensions. He took the opportunity to go to the cinema and contemplate the English Channel waters. The ship took him to another unknown land, where green was ubiquitous. The crossing would take twenty two hours. He would spend one night aboard, with only an extraordinarily large hull supporting him. Everything was new and he absorbed the emotions from that new life. It was like if every breath remained deeply inside his lungs, now free from toxins.

The day broke with land in sight. The small lights of that Celtic land signalled the Atlantic coast. The port of landing was near. Ricardo was anxious to be back on land. He was not fond of the sea and ships. Dry land, where he could walk firmly, was more suitable for him.

A new country was waiting, although most of his time would be spent at the centre.

The group landed and set on their way, among the verdant fields and hills, of an endless green. It was a new spring for Ricardo. He was trying to find himself as a person, to give a new sense to his life. Sometimes he wondered if far from his family and friends, he would see the light that shined on a path that would take him to a more reasonable world, away from drugs. Only time could cure him from that evil life he had taken. He had made his family suffer, as well as himself. It was time to prove that he was stronger than the addiction. There were many residents that could not stand the abstinence, and just ran away from the centres, falling back into drugs. He was determined to end, once and for all, that artificial world that destroyed families and made unscrupulous men rich.

They arrived at the centre after about sixty miles. It was a sunny house, in Irish style, with slate roofs and white-washed walls with brown wooden balconies. They were welcomed by an elder resident, Lucien, French, with about twelve years of association, and his Portuguese wife, very beautiful, who also had been resident for some years.

The centre did not have many activities, as it seemed. The main one was to spread the word around, about the association, in the streets of Irish cities, as it was not quite implanted in Ireland, yet. Through the sale of magazines and direct contact with the population, the intent and responsibility assumed were announced.

There were twenty persons in the centre, with the new group, a mixture of Italians, Spanish, Portuguese, a Norwegian, a Mexican, and the couple in charge. The official language was Spanish, although they were in an English speaking country. It was decided so because of the main incidence of Spaniards in most of the centres all over the world. The founder had created a truly global empire, based on the donations of benefactors. Ricardo wondered about the assets of the association, especially real estates. There were of all kinds, from the modest ones to stately homes.

After settling down at the Irish centre, Ricardo knew that he would be assigned to the animals, since he was a new resident. So, the next morning, after having an English breakfast, he headed to a hill nearby, where the pens were.

He was accompanied by an Italian, a Spaniard, and a woman, also Italian. They took pigswill for two pigs that were being fattened, to be slaughtered, processed and stored in the freezer.

The Irish landscape was idyllic. A refreshing green that stretched to the margins of a river, with a great flow, that reached the Atlantic in two escarpments. All that scenery made Ricardo dream that one day it would be his land. A sentence sounded within his mind: "This is my land!" That thought made his slim body, now recovered from past mistakes, shiver. It could be just a phase, but he wanted to believe that a new life could arise in that enchanted land.

All the residents had different life experiences that, at times, would meet the most absurd of their existence. The Italians were the funniest ones and the most talkative, but they were also the first to go deserted. Life away from society was not easy. It was an enclosed society, actually. Le Patriarche was a different world inside the common world.

Ricardo was preparing to go to town for the first time, to announce the association. The fact of speaking fluent English was an advantage and enabled him to contact with the Irish people. This gave him the opportunity of enjoying the scenery along the way, with three other Portuguese, who had been for longer at the association. The green of the landscape was disconcerting, to the point of boredom.

He intended to give a new meaning to his life. However, he was not sure that he was being successful. He was always wondering about his past. Why did he follow that path? Why had he not been like any ordinary student, without great addictions? His adolescence had been full of excesses. He always lived ahead of the regular. Processes of self affirmation led to personality disorders. The times he had gone to mental health appointments, at his parents' request, the technicians always detected slight mental disturbance. He knew that he had to be medicated, but the association did not allow any chemicals. This was the main divergence between the scientific community and the association supporters. Perhaps, among many other controversies, that was one of the reasons why the French government refused to give support to the association, despite its social nature.

Ricardo started to approach the passer-by in the city streets with a magazine in hand. Most of them ignored him, but there were those who stopped, curious about his figure and silhouette, listened to him and gave a donation.

The day passed by normally, but the city frenzy disturbed him. He had been at the farm for several weeks, without any contact with people from outside the association. The fact of seeing himself all of the sudden engulfed in a crowd and the urban swirl, made him feel tired. He was on the verge of a depression. It was something that did not exist at Le Patriarche.

Ricardo stopped helping at the announcements. He was not in mental health conditions for such task, so he resumed the domestic chores, like animals, kitchen and gardening. The Irish summer was hot. He and other colleagues went often for boat rides in the river. There were moments of leisure despite the arduous work. Water playing offered them refreshment from such a heat.

Every night, group meetings were held after dinner. It was common to talk about a little bit of everything. Ricardo usually remained silent, listening to the elders. All that aura and life philosophy, imposed by the supervisors, had stopped making any sense. Since the beginning, he thought that there was something lurking about the association. He never imagined that one day he would find out the obscurity he presently felt.

A spinster Irish farmer, who lived in the surroundings, used to come by the centre. Her name was Anne and, in one of her visits, she brought a horse with her. Ricardo was amazed with the medium sized equine and he was invited to ride it. Immediately, he mounted on the horse and he was delighted with the small ride. Ricardo knew a little about equitation. He acquired some experience years ago, in a friend's farm. His colleagues and even Anne were amazed with the class and posture he demonstrated, riding the horse. Surely, there were pleasurable moments, despite the hardships faced in the centre.

One morning, unexpectedly, the supervisor decided that the septic tank had to be emptied. So, the residents present at the centre had to get down to business. It was a foul smell. They started to empty that pit of human droppings with some buckets and ropes. They had to take breaks due to inhaled gases. Evidently, there could not be any sewerage in the farm, as it was far from the nearest village. The landscape nearby consisted of hills and fertile valleys, stretching to the river, in the horizon.

Ricardo was getting more and more debilitated as time went by. One night, he was sitting in the doorstep at the entrance, when he started seeing some figures, dressed in white robes with a pointed hat, also white, reminding him of a sect, known for its nefarious effects on society. He was on that hallucinated state for a while. The hallucinations prevailed, keeping him in a condition of constant suffering.

It would soon be his birthday and his colleagues were preparing a cake to celebrate the date. Ricardo could not take care of himself any longer. This began to make the supervisor worried. It was considered the possibility of sending him to a hospital, back in France. Everything was being done without his knowledge. Tomorrow seemed so uncertain. Frequently, instructions were given for activities that were not arranged the day before, like it was supposed to be.

Ricardo was going to leave that land, where he thought he was predestined to live in. His belief had been frustrated. He had never thought that he could get unbalanced. The doctors in his hometown, back in Portugal, had already warned him that he needed to be medicated for the rest of his life. The pathology that he suffered required it. However, Ricardo never took the healthcare technicians advices seriously. His parents tried, without success, to persuade him that he had to follow the doctor's orders. He could not get into excesses and forget the advices he had been told.

There was a certain failure to communicate between families and the residents of the centres. All the conversations were monitored, which generated a latent lack of privacy. The control was very tight. The supervisors were instructed to follow every step given by the new arrivals. Perhaps that was the reason for the high incidence of escapes at the association.

Ricardo said farewell to Ireland, magical land of elves and enchanted realms. He had left behind an unfulfilled dream, a wish that did not come true. Now, he had to return to mainland, where the Patriarche so called health technicians waited for him at Trouville. A centre of excellence where were sent terminal cases of HIV.

The frail mental health of Ricardo worried the supervisors of the Patriarche. It was a rare case of psychic disorder. Evidently, the supervisors dismissed the opinions of technicians from the scientific community. There were presently great controversies in France due to the intransigence of the Patriarche leader and its staff. Ricardo arrived from Ireland completely unbalanced, with a serious depression.

The centre of Trouville was almost like a luxury holiday camp. There was little to do, except for the maintenance of the centre, like cleaning and gardening. On his second day there, Ricardo was taken to the "châteaux", located in front of the other buildings, where the infected and the terminal cases of HIV lived. He was introduced to Marie, a middle-aged Belgian woman, who would give him a relaxing session of massage. It was said that she was an expert in pathological cases of the nervous system. He entered to a room where a massage table was ready for his therapy. A white sheet covered his naked torso and Marie started the session with ambience music. She had beautiful lips, of a mature woman who took good care of herself. Her hands glided over his shoulders, then to his neck and, finally, his nape. Ricardo fell asleep as a result of the relaxing session. Marie placed herself on another massage table, trying to receive his energies and transmit hers. When he woke up, there was no one else in the room, only him and his reasons.

There were moments when Ricardo got completely hallucinated such was his state of debility. Once, while he was smoking a cigarette among the other residents, a German shepherd from the centre was playing with a ball. Ricardo thought that he could intrude into that dog play. When the ball approached, he grabbed it and the dog ran in his direction. Ricardo had the feeling that a crocodile was ready to attack him. The dog crawled with his fur bristled. The hallucination caused him to panic. All that debility and unbalanced state worried the supervisors of the centre, who did not know how to cope with the situation.

Ricardo woke up a certain day in the morning and dressed a red ski suit, believing that he was an astronaut. He walked slowly, as if there was no gravity at the centre. The kitchen and the noise from the extractor made him think that there it was a space ship ready to take-off into orbit. Ricardo was totally immersed in a world of fantasy, apart from reality. Sometimes, when cleaning the "châteaux", after he descended the exotic wooden centenary staircases, he sprayed them to erase all the traces of his footsteps, although they did not exist. His colleagues remained incredulous with his behaviour.

He had always been traumatized and marked by those infected with HIV, who had special treatment. At some point, he started to have dinner at the "châteaux", together with the HIV infected in terminal phase. There were three women at the table, with very deformed faces, an evidence of the deadly disease. Marie was also there and looked in awe at Ricardo. He had a plate of spaghetti Bolognese in front of him, looking good, but he did not have any appetite. Ricardo observed those faces, martyred by a disease about which little was known, but that was killing young men and women mercilessly.

He handled well with the HIV-positives situation, although some caution was required, especially when going to the bathroom. The fresh blood from shaving cuts could be a serious focus of infection. Some of his colleagues at the centre turned to him and used to say: - "It's AIDS!" And he watched the blood in the lavatories that others left unclean by carelessness. There were also rules of hygiene imposed by the supervisors, such as the disinfection of cutlery from the canteen, which were cleaned with bleach every time they were used.

Eight months had gone by since he had left Portugal. After passing through several centres and different experiences, his health was decaying increasingly. He no longer was living in a real world. His mind was in permanent conflict with his conscience. His parents were extremely worried, but could not find a solution to bring him back home. The supervisors of the centre wanted him to stay because he was a source of income to the association. At the time of admission it was usually told that the program lasted for a year. However, in fact, things did not happen that way. The residents did not have freedom of choice to leave whenever they wanted. They were brainwashed by the supervisors, who claimed that they were not prepared to be reinstated in society and they would relapse. The residents could not carry their identification cards as they were withheld by the supervisors. Only the elders and those who went outside could have it. Some people connected the association with a criminal organization, because many were there to avoid jail.

Ricardo felt very often bitterness for what he was going through, but it had been his past life that led him to that situation. No one but himself could be blamed for his condition. His parents did everything they could to free him from drugs. This was supposed to be the end of the line. It was time for a new life for him and his family's sake.

All along his permanence at the association he had slowly fallen to the present state of degradation, making his stay unsustainable. Psychological therapy was the main point of disagreement. Chemical medication was not allowed for the psychiatric treatment. Furthermore, the staff of Patriarche did not recognise the existence of psychiatric problems. They were a result of each one's imagination. The scientific community repudiated and denounced the treatments practiced at the association. It could be said that the Patriarche lived behind closed doors that were only opened to announce its successes.

Trouville kept the final memories. Perhaps it was the end of the line of all the drug rehabilitation process. Ricardo remembered in his moments of lucidity all the months he had spent there. Since his admission at Narbonne, he had been disappointed with the effectiveness of the association. The Patriarche was not prepared for his pathology. A change was needed in terms of psychiatric illnesses. It was mandatory to overcome the taboo of the use of chemicals. If the infected with HIV could ingest chemicals to fight the disease, why should not the mentally ill?

The founder of the association was unyielding, leading to a discredit before the scientific community. The French society regarded them as a band of criminals, where many joined to avoid being arrested.

There was, for sure, a great empire of realty. Some were donations, like farms and stately homes. No one knew for certain how they had been acquired or in which context.

Ricardo wanted to leave the association, but the supervisors said that he was not prepared to be reinstated in society. As a matter of fact, each day, his mental health provoked new psychotic episodes.

When his parents asked about him, they were always told that he was fine. Nevertheless, when he talked to his mother, he used to say that he did not feel well and he wanted to go back to Portugal.

Definitely, that was not his world, nor the Irish land that he thought as his. He had to be treated in Portugal as he needed appropriate medication.

On the other hand, not everything was bad about the association. It took in people that followed a righteous path. People with no relatives found shelter and, sometimes, even a new family inside. The wealthy and those who could afford paid for the less fortunate. There was a social nature in the association philosophy, for sure. However, the residents were retained by persistence, many times against their will.

Going back through recent times, when together with other residents, Ricardo felt that he had experienced happy moments. The football games in Narbonne, where he displayed his talent. The boat rides in the Irish river that made him feel one with Nature. The games with the girls, like the hose baths in the summer heat. All those reminiscences would last for a lifetime.

He left Portugal eight months ago and that was too much time without his medication. His brain became more fragile day after day. He could no longer keep up with the activities. In his last days at Trouville, Victor, a Portuguese elder, was in charge of him. He had the task of forcing Ricardo to eat, since he could barely feed himself. The depression was taking over him and Victor was in a thorny issue.

The kitchen and the extractors gave him the hallucination of a spaceship ready to take-off. Whenever he heard the noise, he travelled in time, caught in the whirlwind of his imagination. Obviously, he did not share his hallucinations with anyone. He was enclosed in his world. That entire extravaganza performed by him made the other residents feel confused. The red ski suit in the summer was weird. The slow motion steps through the tiled floors of the centre made everyone else feel awkward, desperate to go back home.

The experience lived by Ricardo at that excellence centre would predict that his return home was imminent. At that time, his family and the supervisors of the Patriarche were in a tug of war to have him sent back to Portugal. A threat was made by his family of denouncing the case to the French television if he was not freed by the centre. Ricardo was kept in the dark from these backstage talks.

Since his admission in Coimbra, with the presence of a social worker, a scenario of cordiality had been displayed by the association. It had a credible status at the eyes of Portuguese society. There was some secrecy among the managers and everything was made by negotiations with them.

Ricardo had been through moments of nostalgia and frail physical condition. He had learnt that there are moments in life when we cannot count on our own, we are dependent on others. The more he fought against the tide, the more he had to suffer the constraints resultant from his past life.

Le Patriarche would go on and he would be one among the thousands of young men and women who had been there. His case had been different, but many others happened in different contexts.

He did not keep many memories and affinities from his resident colleagues at the association. He had been especially touched by the HIV-positives who fought for a dignified life, knowing that they would have a different destiny than his. It was a fight against a predestined time to a premature death.

The gardens he planted in Narbonne. The whitewashed walls painted by him and the affection to the animals he had cared in Ireland would mark his life. He had also left good references among the friends he had made there. Certainly, he would never see those people again. He would take on his memory an interchange of life-stories, based on their small existence together, a knowledge that he would carry on forever.

The community concept of Le Patriarche was interesting. Equality of rights and opportunities were the foundations, however, the hierarchy enjoyed certain privileges that they tried to hide from the remaining residents. The "sevrages", new residents during the adaptation period, were dealt as fragile people needing special support. The elders, residents with more than six to eight years of association, enjoyed some autonomy but with increased responsibility. No one knew for sure what was stirring in the minds of the supervisors. Sometimes, decisions were made hastily, like if the others had to be ready for any type of action.

When Ricardo was peacefully taking care of the animals at the Irish centre, all of the sudden, a group arrived, coming from France. They were residents specialised in building construction. They came to restore a house, property of the founder of the association, located close to the centre and at the same time, restore the centre where Ricardo was. He remembered seeing a huge HGV, carried with construction supplies that required unloading. It was not easy for Ricardo to carry, on his back, with 110 pounds cement bags for an hour. Jaded, when he got to the centre by night, he did not have dinner. He went straight to bed without even taking a shower. He was completely exhausted. By 7:30 a.m. he got up, took a shower, dressed up and immediately seemed like if the house was falling down. The bricklayer's mates were demolishing the bathrooms upstairs and the kitchen was in rubble. Ricardo did not know what they were doing. At lunch that had been made in the courtyard, he overheard a conversation from a supervisor about him. He was saying that Ricardo needed to be taken to Trouville, which was the best place to be treated. Thus, he got to know that some supervisors came to Ireland with instructions to take him back to mainland.

Ricardo was still assimilating everything presently. The more he was told that he had to react, or as they like to put it: "stark raving mad", all his involvement in activities started to fade. The entire process of psychological regression, with chronic psychosis pathology, aggravated over the time due to the medicines abstinence. His relatives would still try to convince the supervisors to administrate his medication. Nevertheless, their appeals fell on deaf ears.

His relocation to Ireland might have been the trigger to the psychological conflict within his mind. While in Narbonne, life would have proceeded as usual. Yet little time had passed since he had left the medication.

Could Ricardo escape from the centre? Surely he could do so, turning himself in to the police, but he never tried. It never crossed his mind to escape, despite watching many running away, even people with more time than him.

It was complicated. The image that the supervisors of the centres intended on showing to the society did not correspond with the reality in the association. Many prevailing factors on the day-to-day running of the centres, namely in the rural areas, far from everyone and everything, were omitted. There was a thing in common between all the centres. The supervisors could be proud about the hygiene that was here, there and everywhere. Everything was cleaned and disinfected properly. It could not be otherwise, with so many HIV-positives it might become a great source of infection.

It was never heard of an audit to the operating conditions and licensing of the association by the official authorities. Perhaps, because it was private, there was not great rigour in the institutional monitoring. It was known that the police frequently checked the centres and, very often, certain residents were hidden.

Nobody was alone at the association, unless the elders, who enjoyed certain privileges. Everyone should be accompanied, in pairs or even in groups. It was an important rule. The fact of being alone could lead to improper thoughts and not obtaining immediate assistance.

Ricardo rarely spoke at group meetings, as he believed that it did not make any sense. Exposing his deepest feelings to people that he barely knew was not in his character. He felt only available to discuss about work problems at the centre. He used to serve as an interpreter of English to some Germans and Nordics who did not speak Spanish.

Ricardo had not made any special friend. The only exception had been Paulo, the driver from Narbonne, who had picked him to be his mate for the cargo deliveries around southern France. Life seemed to make another sense those days he had spent with Paulo. There was freedom of movements, without being watched by others. He felt free and that was very important for him. The lack of freedom trapped his soul. But he also knew that he was there to redeem from his past. He did not know in which conditions he had been admitted, but probably for a year. All the residents had trouble in leaving the centres.

During his vague ramblings, Ricardo had one thing for sure. The association was inadequate to his way of being. It might have been a learning process and a rewarding experience, however many other aspects were disappointing. The entire rehabilitation process was jeopardized by the absence of autonomy, free decision and liberty to express controversial feelings.

Although psychologically debilitated, Ricardo could still display his excellent guitar skills. He borrowed one off a colleague. Alone with Paulo, in the common room, he played a surprising theme that he composed. The sound echoed through the hall, clear, and absorbed Paulo, completely. He plucked the guitar like if it was an announcement of his departure. Even he was surprised with his musical improvisation. There were moments that would stay forever engraved in his memories.

Trouville was a hospital and a reinsertion centre. He only got to know this later, when Paulo and an Italian woman took him to the Orly airport.

Life was not going well for him. The hallucinations remained frequent. Still, he had moments of lucidity and sharing with his colleagues. He talked about Portugal, his hometown, the marginalization and the lack of support from the Portuguese institutions. He used to say that he did not know what was going on with him. The esoteric thoughts were stronger than his will to lead a normal life. From bricklayer's mate, gardener, farmer, cook, he was a little bit of everything. He became acquainted with other cultures and learnt what it is to be a Patriarche. The lack of psychiatric support for his depression was the drop that made the vase overflow. Nothing could be done about it. The administration was intransigent, due to the stubbornness of the founder. He insisted on a natural cure for all ills, whether physical or psychological.

Le Patriarche was, in fact, a great real estate empire that resorted to free labour. Almost everything came from donations, recollected by the residents with trucks and vans from the association. There was cash flow from the monthly fees of the residents. Most of the fixed expenditures, like bread, water, electricity, gas and fuels had to be covered by donations and the monthly fees.

Ricardo, in his naivety, believed, after his arrival at the association, that it developed a great social service in favour of mankind. Later, however, it turned out that was classified as a sect by part of the world press. He did not share this view. He thought that the association had merit in its work of rehabilitating drug addicts. At least, while there, they did not consume any drugs or alcohol. And they had time to think about what they wanted to do with their lives.

When Ricardo arrived at the centre in Narbonne, he was clean for two and a half months. He had gone on his own, without the need of any family, contrary to the usual. On the other hand, his situation took a turn to the worst. The absence of medication unbalanced him. Matters aggravated both for him as for the supervisors of the centres where he had been.

Le Patriarche was a life style, free of drugs or alcohol. It meant standing together and helping each other. This was made according to previously defined methods. It was known that there were gaps at the association, like the elders privileges. It was understandable due to the high level of confidence they had acquired over the years. Life without drugs or alcohol was a hard task for some residents, who did not fit in properly. The cold beer in a hot day was sorely missed. Some residents, with enough time to go announcing the association, suffered a relapse and got into alcohol. They had to start all over again, going back to "sevrage".

Ricardo followed the rules of the centres without questioning too much. He knew that there was no other alternative unless to obey them. The greatest worry for him was the inexistence of a date to be released from the association. The retention of residents had originated some polemic in the society. When he knew that not even in two or three years he would be able to leave, he panicked. On his way to Ireland, he was no longer sure that he could ever return home. This rule led to the escape of many residents.

Once a month, Ricardo was allowed to talk to his family. The phone calls lasted only three minutes, always monitored by a supervisor of the centre. This was a mean of dissuading residents from complaining to their families. Ricardo found that unacceptable, a total lack of privacy. But, what could be done? That was how things worked. Of course, that detail had been omitted at the time of his admission. It was all like the proverbial rose garden. Many joyful moments at the centres, sometimes, turned into sadness. Several residents could not handle with the feeling of isolation and became stark raving mad.

Ricardo was torn between the uncertainty of a definitive cure and a state of upheaval within. He wondered how he came to that situation. He could not understand the many mistakes he had made along his life and all the years of drug addiction. He had many other healthier pleasures in life that he had started to discover. Maybe Le Patriarche was a ticket for a new life. He finally understood that many others like him wanted to leave drugs through the association.

According to the administration, the rate of success in the rehabilitation process was seventy percent. On the other hand, there were reasons to believe that it was lower than that. It cannot really be said that there was reinsertion in society. Their goal was to keep the residents in the association, some for the secured income and others for the free workforce.

Half of the nine months that Ricardo spent at the association were marked by the deterioration of his mental health. The absence of medication to his condition led to an extreme debility. The heavy physical labour, on its own, did not do much for his deranged state. This was the point where the founder's philosophy failed miserably. The scientific community warned about this issue. They were called a sect by the international press. Moreover, the founder was not as altruistic as he pretended to be. There were legal proceedings in courts, with criminal convictions of several degrees. He was even demanded by justice. The last period of his life he sought refuge in Belize. The community's ideology was rather interesting, still, over the years, developed such proportions that changed its course.

The last period of Ricardo in the association was of utter suffering. His colleagues could not imagine such a strong feeling of sadness. But everything pointed to an imminent departure from the association. All the expectations that, either way, they had put in that community had became frustrated. His mother was disappointed. She did not expect such intransigence from the association supervisors. One of her cousins went all the way and issued an ultimatum.

There was some fundamentalism in the rules applied. Ever since its foundation, when everything was simpler and admission was less strict, the altruistic values were left behind. At the same time as it gained proportion, it became a profitable business, both financial as in real estate.

Ricardo felt nostalgic during all his stay at the Trouville centre. Psychologically debilitated and far too sensitive, he watched the faces of his companions. Sad faces, miserable and willing to be with their families again. Relatives could only visit after a very long permanence and pending on their good behaviour reviews.

Ricardo faced the HIV-positives not with despise nor reluctance, but with sadness. He observed the disease marks on their bodies tormented by that fatal creature, which took lives indiscriminately. The negatives had to ward off infection, since they all live together. The bathrooms were the places with greatest risk. They were disinfected everyday to avoid contamination.

Le Patriarche could be a safe haven for the HIV-positives that enjoyed yearningly for life, but it was also a refuge for criminals in hiding from police authorities. Ricardo witnessed, many times, episodes when residents were hidden... Only the administration was aware of the criminal records. It was mandatory to submit one, along with clinical analysis, at the time of admission. The association was very well organised. All of the staff was composed of former drug addicts.

Ricardo was living in a constant uncertainty. He had no future projects. He was waiting for the events to unfold only hoping to go back home with his family. All his expectations had been frustrated. What had looked like a bright future for him has revealed a true nightmare. Twelve hundred miles from home, he could not find a way of returning to his native land, where the family warmth might open up new horizons. He would not find safety among his former group of friends, evidently. He would need to cut off with drinking or drug using buddies. Life had given him wings to fly, but he had soared too high. Somewhere along the flight, he fell into vice.

Le Patriarche proclaimed a life free from drugs. That, alone, was not enough. Reinsertion was imperative but it did not exist. It was merely misleading advertising. The guidelines of the administration were to retain residents for an indefinite period. For all its merits, the association would always have a deficit of freedom to decide and act.

Twenty three years after having gone through the association, Ricardo looks back at it as a learning experience in his life. At the time, he was still young, without any projects for his future. The impulsiveness of youth had left reminiscences of uncertain times and too much oblivious craziness. He also recalled good joyful convivial moments. After surviving to such difficult times, he is now aware that his life could have taken a more perilous course. He lost many friends along the way. Those premature deaths, whose remembrance, would mark him forever. Lives, that had suffered much more than him. Never questioning that, he had tried to be as understanding as he could.

After leaving the association, Ricardo never saw again anyone from the thousands of colleagues that had also been there. It was a period of his life, crossroads gone by, that he keeps with no anger towards the supervisors. At least, he had never been mistreated nor physically abused. The only downside had been his retention at the centre and the absence of the medication required to treat his mental health problem.

Ricardo still evokes his days at the Narbonne centre, gardening. He planted two dozens of small cedars in the patio. He would like to return there, someday and see the results of his work. Observe how much they have grown, giving a new image to the complex.

In all the time he spent at the association, he never fell in love for any girl. There were a few beautiful young women at the centres. The most beautiful were in couple, the remaining lived in harmony with their male colleagues. There was not great harassment to the girls, especially because it was forbidden. He was called, sometimes, Manuel, or Manu, depending on the centres. It used to happen to the most popular people when changing between centres. He still remembers some of the girls, like a Norwegian named Anne, an Italian, or even the Portuguese Paula, who welcomed him on his admission.

Everything was ephemeral during his stay at the association. The faces, some of them happy while other sad. The messages he was told, according to the will of the moment. The instruction he had received in each centre could be beneficial. Moreover, he memorised the signs that emphasised his condition of being in recovery. These experiences were taken as a future memory. Being isolated from the rest of society was not enough, as was known to Ricardo. A community inside a more adverse one might not have been the solution to his problems. But, back then, it could not have been otherwise. He accepted that condition and subjected to it, even transitorily.

Le Patriarche would always be seen, by the French society, as a gang of criminals, trying to redeem themselves from past mistakes. The organisational structure was well established so that nothing could fail. The logistics worked accordingly to its goals. Ricardo used to think of it like a huge monster, with tentacles expanding all over the world.

While staying in Celtic lands, Ricardo had the chance to meet an Irish farmer called Anne, who went to the centre frequently. She was a rude looking spinster, yet very feminine, that lived nearby. She looked like a woman who fought very hard through her life. Maybe she felt lonely in her farm and enjoyed the company of the residents of the centre. Her goats used to run away to the centre and, suddenly, she appeared, with her dog, relentlessly gathering the flock. The goats destroyed very often the shale walls of the centre. The supervisors reproached it. They had to rebuild the walls many times. Nevertheless, they had all the time in the world. It was like a therapy for the negative thoughts that haunted the residents every second.

Ricardo enjoyed a lot the boat rides along the river, stopping in the banks, where they would visit beautiful woods that reminded him of medieval tales. In these moments the world became different. It was imperative to break the monotony of the centre and to forget the isolation they were subjected to. The elder elements that had some autonomy, made all the necessary arrangements. When new individuals arrived at the group, things got complicated. The attentions were drawn to them, carefully so not to cause any stress facing the new reality.

Actually, there was a great mutual help between the residents. Each one had a different life experience that set him apart from the others. In common, they had the commitment to help their neighbours. Ricardo shared these views except in what regarded to group meetings. He believed that he had little to say to his colleagues. Sometimes, he served as a translator for a German. He had to intervene to call his attention to the clothes that needed to be kept in the right places. Everything was well organised, there was not any anarchy at the centres. Even though they were a sharing community, there was a method to it. Only this way, with a well defined structure, the association could succeed.

While in his lucid state, Ricardo wanted to believe that his problems with drugs were going to be solved, but he was not quite sure of himself. The greatest issue would be the return to his hometown and confront with former drug abuse buddies. Since there was no reinsertion policy, it would be hard to leave the hypothetical program unfinished. However, his poor mental state, while at Trouville, did not allow him to get around the point. It was urgent to handle his repatriation. His family had already been arranging it, without his knowledge.

At Trouville, Ricardo kept hallucinating that he was boarding the space ship that was about to take-off to an unknown destination. The noise from the extractors made him shiver due to the innermost desire of liberation from his woes. In his last days at the centre, he kept wearing the red ski suit with blue tennis. In slow motion steps he strolled around the centre like if he was training to embark in a space odyssey. Without the antidote to strengthen and keep him lucid, his mind was in a serious state of fragility. No one managed to follow him such was his aplomb. Since he was not dangerous, nor aggressive, the supervisors let him wander around in his delusions. Every time a resident died, victim of HIV, a fundraiser was made to buy a floral wreath. In the last funeral, Ricardo donated all of his money, even not knowing the deceased very well. This gesture surprised everyone. He felt it almost as an obligation to his spirit, even though he had nothing to do with the situation. He believed it was a way of showing that he was sympathetic with his infected colleagues, despite he was negative.

The HIV-positives had privileges, as they were the most sensitive group and the ones who required more attention, so it was understandable.

In the early days of the association, the residents could drink wine at meals. At least, that is what he was told. In the beginning, all excluded from society, like homeless and marginal were accepted by the founder. Over time it took a disparate course. In the eighties, the social situation was quite different. The HIV was still largely unknown. There were not many infected. It became a priority for the association over the years due to serious risk behaviour. The drug addicts, without the perspectives of a treatment, started dying too soon.

Ricardo, at the start of his admission, was a little afraid of living together with the HIV-positives. But as time went by he realised there were no problems whatsoever. Both sides assumed precautions to avoid infections and, in fact, there were few reports of such cases. "Mariages" were celebrated between positives and negatives, who acknowledged their sexual limitations. That communal world was unthinkable in the society, thus the political and governmental warnings.

Narbonne, Chartres, Cork and Trouville would remain forever recorded in Ricardo's memories as one of the most complex experience of his life. Before his admission to the association, a meeting occurred at the hospital where Ricardo was in, between him, his family, the social assistant and two representatives of Le Patriarche. If anyone told him what was going to happen, he would not have ever believed it. Le Patriarche was introduced by the representatives almost as a holiday camp, where residents lived happily. That was not the reality. Ricardo feels glad for overcoming, with the help of his family, that obstacle in his life. Le Patriarche had supported many people, but in his case, it had been a setback. The association was a safe haven for many drug addicts who wished to abandon the vice and a life of crime. Youths from dysfunctional families sought refuge in the association for an undetermined period to reorganise their lives. Most lived on the streets, depending on usually illicit schemes and had drug misfortunes.

Ricardo did not condemn the founder neither the supervisors of the association. From his own experience, he knew that the absence of chemicals in the treatment was an unacceptable gap. In his particular case, the problem could not be solved by weariness and herbal infusions. It was counterproductive to measure everything by the same yardstick. Some cases had a diagnosed pathology, such as schizophrenia, chronic psychoses or even bipolar disorder.

Ricardo often perceived certain arrogance by the people in charge of each nationality group. They would use their power in the association to pour out their frustrations. Ricardo had never witnessed a physical aggression on his colleagues by the supervisors although in Cork, a Portuguese was assaulted with a headbutt. However, this happened in private and the real reasons were never known. Everything pointed to an action of passionate nature. Furthermore, people became more docile the longer the permanence in the association. There was no apology to violence.

Ricardo looks back to his times at the association, two decades later, with serenity and no hard feelings. His addiction to drugs had taken him there. But he brought with him teachings for life. He learned how to cook Italian food, to kill ducks and to process them to freeze, and also how to paint. Besides, he acquired a sense of solidarity among Men.

No one can state that a tabula rasa should be made from what was going on in the association. It also had some virtues. Although its founder had been corrupt and wanted by justice, it does not invalidate the beneficence effort and dedication of many supervisors, who had nothing to do with the founders' obscure businesses and eccentric behaviour. The enclosed character of the association caused weirdness in society. Still there was no other way of fighting drug abuse, unless with isolation from the adversities and temptations of society.

Up to the point of his mental breakdown, Ricardo's recovery was according to the association prospects. He might not agree with certain rules, but since he had accepted the terms and conditions of admission, he calmly followed the instructions given by the supervisors. He was under a great psychological strain, provoked by the lack of the medication that was not allowed by the association. Ricardo tried to fight off his mind's decompensation. Sometimes, he travelled in the present through delirium that tormented his soul. Definitely, this was not a place for him.

The short trip he had made with the Portuguese Paulo, in Narbonne, in order to deliver and collect food, made him feel like if a new life had come. He had covered several cities in the Mediterranean coast, always listening to music from the cassette player. Hard Rock, mainly Guns n' Roses, that was Paulo's favourite band. The beaches would appear in a turquoise sea that filled his soul. The weather felt like summer, warmed by the wind of "Suão" that blew in the sunny morning. He wished that those moments could last forever. As expected, this only lasted two days. The arrival at the centre was like returning to the gloom of isolation, as a punishment for past mistakes.

Ricardo was a small talking young man, extremely observer and good listener. He heard the most amazing stories that his friends got off their chests in moments of great weakness. In those days, there were not social networks and everything was face to face. The power of the media was centred in television and the written press. Only supervisors had access to outside news, who did not share it with the residents for internal security reasons. That world turned around its own axis. Every unorthodox movement by the residents were detected and analysed step by step. No one could desert, but sometimes it happened. On some occasions they were caught, others not. When this took place, they would go through rough moments in questioning. As they used to say, they had to "face the music" and, everyday, were assigned the hardest tasks to those that broke the rules.

The retention of the residents was a result of the association's authoritarianism. Those who commit infractions were set aside and looked upon as persona non grata.

Since the green fields of Ireland, where freedom seemed more tangible, Ricardo had lost all sense of psychological independence. When he had returned from Celtic lands, he had already been much debilitated. He could barely remember crossing the channel aboard the ferry boat. The only thing he could remember was being brought by two Portuguese, coming to mainland. Their mission in Ireland had finished and they accompanied Ricardo to

Trouville. Here, the gardens were well kept. The long bushes, nicely shaped and pruned, allowed fresh walks and to contemplate the blooming flowers. He recalled the staircases inside the sunny manor house. They were in African Blackwood, well preserved. The building was probably from the late seventeenth century. It still retained all of the initial structure, only suffering small conservation interventions. The association or its founder, managed that many old buildings were donated them and later restored. The real estates of the association were worth a great fortune. It was never known who, after the founder's recent death, had become his trustee.

The residents endured, among the scams and solidarity. It was their monetary contributions, at least of most of them that continued to support the association. Nowadays, there are many therapeutic communities, some with methods even more unorthodox than Le Patriarche.

Ricardo believed that he would never see his family again. He was trapped in that enclosed environment where the outside world looked, frequently, like a mirage. The girls were few and he could not perceive any as a possible partner for that journey of recovery from life's misfortunes. Moreover, he was not in the mood for romance, neither it was viable such was the control over them. He wanted to solve his drug addiction problem. He intended to return to his hometown, as a new man, with future projects for his life. Otherwise, his mental health was getting worse, day after day. He was only a step away from madness. Without realising it, he was on the edge of sanity, about to lose it.

The organisation of Le Patriarche as a whole was a closed circle. Few elements came from outside the association in order to work together. The social security regularly referred this association to families with problems, as a way of discarding responsibilities. Every case of drug addiction is of an enormously difficult resolution. Commonly, only with maturity it is possible to achieve a drug-free life. The conscience of living without drugs must come from within and Le Patriarche could not do that for anyone.

Ricardo had no conviction that the moment had come to quit drugs permanently. Some years later he saw the light, when the ground was cut under his feet. Then, he finally decided it was time to stay clean from drugs for once and for all. His passage by the association had been a learning phase, undoubtedly. It was like a sign that a radical divide was necessary to his life, clearing away from drugs.

Deep down, Ricardo felt lonely among the many residents that also had their own emotional issues. The remembrance of his small hometown, where life went on normally, was always on his mind. He had no knowledge of what was going on there. He did not care about the conflicts in the association. They did not matter for his endeavours. He knew of the existence of vested interests among the supervisors. But, he never went any farther than the rumours that were circulating intramural. Every time someone broke the rules of the centres, it was usual to administer punishments. They consisted, normally, in tending the animals for one week: pigs, chickens, ducks, etc. Nobody liked to remove the droppings, but someone had to do it. Another usual punishment was a week in the kitchen, washing large pans that could be used to cook for a regiment. Precisely, in these situations, sometimes, escapes were prompted from the centres. Stuck for endless days in forced labour, they could not cope with the pressure. Eventually, they deserted turning themselves in to the police authorities of the nearest town. Sometimes, the supervisors went after them. When captured, they were brainwashed and, few days later, transferred to another centre, even against their will.

It can be said that the community was ruled under a certain dictatorship of decisions. The residents had no vote in matters that were of their interest. A despotic hierarchy existed that made all decisions without consulting the residents.

Amidst that strict discipline, one thing was for certain, individuals without social methods and rules would regain them. Good practices such as hygiene habits, caring for their clothes, daily shower and keeping their rooms clean. No one could take the merit of the association for that. As for the rest, there were pertinent questions from those outside the association. The international press has always considered it as a sect of recovering drug abusers, due to the system they had developed.

While in Ireland, Ricardo had written letters to a friend talking about the centre like if it was an oasis in the association. Spring had arrived, lush green, and flowers covered the fields beautifully. He used to say in an impassioned tone that he might have Celtic origin. In a meeting with a priest from Cork, who supported youths in poor economical condition, they were introduced to two Irish young girls of celestial beauty. One was redhead and the other blond, both with freckles and peaceful souls that inspired anyone.

On June 26, the International Day against Drug Abuse and Illicit Trafficking, Ricardo went to the streets of Cork to spread the word about the association. He took with him some magazines to sell. Among the crowd that roamed the streets he managed to sell some, at the same time, he explained the day-to-day running of the association. He had already a well rehearsed talk, so he had no actual need to think about its content. However, this activity did not last long for him. Immediately, on his second time, he started feeling depressed. He could not even speak. He simply wandered aimlessly around the streets, with the magazines in his hands. His Portuguese colleagues that were in the group started to think that his behaviour was odd. From that day on, Ricardo was never again assigned to that task. He was held at the centre until the arrival of a new team, when the supervisor decided to send him back to mainland. He had no medication for six months and the triggering of his crisis started to evince its signs. It could have been a depression or not. The fact remains that there was no other option than to send him back to France. There, at the referred hospital of the association, in Trouville, his case would be followed. Yet this hypothetical hospital only had palliative care for HIV patients. It did not have a psychiatric service.

The all concept of work in order to cause physical fatigue it was not generally successful. There were residents like Ricardo suffering from mental health disorders. Although in small numbers, they were on the verge of madness. The methodology applied in the treatment of drug addicts might be viable, but there were gaps that the founder and the administration of the association were not determined to rectify. Having thousands in rehabilitation was an achievement for the association. What would be the price to pay for any errors?

It was a fact that the permanence at the association made residents lose their folly, which had been induced by drug abuse. A sense of responsibility was acquired, as well as hygiene routines and discipline in performing the tasks. It is true and nobody can deny it. Nevertheless, the most important issue about all the process was: - How long it was required to attain freedom of action in regard to society?

Ricardo never found out due to his early exit. According to testimonies of colleagues who were living there for over a year, he was made to believe that the retention of residents was merely for economic reasons.

It cannot be stated that after a year they were completely healed. The cure was always an uncertainty. Even though Ricardo was free from drugs a long time ago, others relapsed after five or six years. Each case was unique. There were also stories of success. Youths that ascertained the truth and after many awareness meetings came down to earth and broke the chains that tied them to that artificial world that disgraced families.

All this theory of addictions recovery was based in a communal life philosophy and commitment to work, as a way of setting aside any tendency to deviance with evil intentions.

Over the entire recovery process, Ricardo became aware that drugs were not the way of life he intended for him. Through all the adversities, his family was always a safe harbour, never giving up on his deliverance from drugs. They believed that one day it would be possible, even if he was in a pitch dark, bottomless pit. At that point, the family support would be important in his emergence to a new life, more healthy and ready to accept responsibilities before society. Ricardo's parents were fighters, indefatigable warriors. They had always been hopeful and believed that he would rehabilitate.

Le Patriarche was, for many, a model of drug rehabilitation that housed homeless people, men running from justice, mere drug addicts and alcoholics. Actually, it was a place where a community of individuals, who were marginalised by society, lived in coexistence, sharing equally without regarding to backgrounds. This was about the common resident because, as it has already been mentioned, the supervisors had certain exclusive privileges.

Ricardo experienced moments of pure delight, especially in Ireland, while still in possession of all his mental faculties. The green fields were inviting for strolls through endless prairies, climbing hills, from where he enjoyed the oversight of the meanderings of a river. And the thought "This is my Land!" obfuscated his mind, but it was clearly just a dream that he could hardly fulfil. His homeland was in fact Portugal, where he grew up. It was there that he had to start a new life, free from the ordeals of drugs. He had always covered winding paths, easily attracted by adventure, without thinking about the implications. Thus, he had been setting out strong roots for a frail existence.

Many years had gone by since Ricardo had left the association. He was curious to see the centres where he had been, now in a more critical and coherent way. He would like to know the present rituals and how the association was structured today, after the death of its founder. Perhaps some methods had been changed. Or, as it was more likely, the workings are still the same.

His past life had taught him to mature gradually, on its own time. Le Patriarche was, actually, a reference to many people, particularly those with scarce resources in order to give up on drugs. Albeit the success rate for short term treatment was very low, it provided a safe haven for many youths to reflect upon their lives.

Some facts were far beyond his understanding. The elites of the association led lives that did not match the established practices. There were cars at their disposal and they could walk alone around the centres, as well. This was unthinkable for most of the residents. The elders had a distinct position, which, sometimes, caused a feeling of unease among the other residents. If deep down that was a community with equal rights, these privileged members were a violation.

It is known that there are no ideal societies. However, it would be positive that such a small community could follow the grounds imposed by its founder.

Ricardo had been through hard times at the association, as well as good moments. Yet, definitely, this would not be the perfect place for him. His psychological structure could not fit in the psycho-pedagogic rules enforced by the supervisors. He still tried, without success, to persuade them to give him permission to resume his prior medication. They were absolutely inflexible about it. He could not accept their discrimination. Why could the HIV-positives take chemicals and could he not have his brain medication?

The scientific community did not agree with these methods. They rejected all forms of treatment that did not take in consideration the particularities of each individual. Everyone has a different psychological structure. Each of us is unique which leads to specific treatments. However, when Ricardo arrived to Trouville, his world had already been out of step with reality. His psychological disorder was such that few residents managed to support him through his delusions. He used to wander alone around the centre and nobody bothered him.

When B52 bombers crossed the skies over Trouville, he believed that a war was raging the world. In his mind, a world war broke out, this time it was against space invaders from outer planet. He had no idea how they were, but imagined that a space ship was in the centre ready to take-off and few residents would travel aboard. He was one of the chosen to flee from the cataclysm the world was in. Then, as if nothing had happened, he went back to normal and forgot those psychotic hallucinations.

The talks between Ricardo's family and the leaders of the association, concerning his release from the centre and immediate return home, were nearly complete. All that was left was to book the flight from Orly that would take him to Portugal. The negotiations were hard. His family had been willing to denounce the case to the French television channels. This would have forced, sooner or later, the French authorities to take action. The leaders of the association, facing the facts, had no other choice but to give in, for it could be assumed as kidnapping of a foreign citizen.

Ricardo was kept in the dark of all these matters. His dementia was in a stage that he could no longer tell right from wrong.

Many years later and in sound mental health, he told me that, deep down, he did not recognise a remarkable merit in the therapeutic processes of the association. He mentioned that it was more like a shelter for those seeking refuge from justice due to drug-related questions. He also told me that these niches of unconventional therapeutics were allowed by society, as well as authorities, in order to get rid of delinquency.

There are those who praise the association and its merits and they have the right to do it. Nonetheless, Ricardo, who had spent nine months in several centres, did not share this view. Perhaps, with the death of its founder, a wider overture to the scientific community might be possible.

All the pleasant moments that Ricardo experienced in Le Patriarche, were not enough for him to have a positive outcome from the time he was there. Ricardo's drug addiction was not over until some months later when, in Portugal, he had a relapse. Yet, he managed to prove that the scientific therapeutic methods are more effective in cases of mental disorders.

Two decades have passed since the last time he consumed drugs. Nowadays, he looks back at that past as a troubled period he had experienced. At just the right time of his life, he knew how to put an end to that situation.

In life, we have to learn to seize the right moment in order to avoid meaningless existences. It is imperative to get real and be aware that there is a life beyond drugs that is much more advantageous and happy, despite all adversities.

The process of maturing and the weight carried by those years led Ricardo to do a deep introspection of his experience with drugs. He came to the conclusion that nothing makes sense in that world, nothing at all. Not even the moments of euphoria and artificial pleasure generated by drugs. Beyond sorting out his addiction, he also knew how to deal with his mental disorder. He was clever enough to understand how to take action against the daily excesses and tiredness.

If Le Patriarche was in fact that good, instead of having some thousands of persons in treatment, they would have millions all over the world. The communal concept of living without drugs had many gaps as mentioned before.

Today, Ricardo does not like to attend places where drugs are consumed, not even a simple joint. Definitely, this is not his world. It causes him anguish to see youths, as he once was, living in that tragic world. He does not discriminate anyone for being drug addicts. He just does not want to socialise with them, especially because it brings him echoes of a time past. A period, in which he lost many of the good things in life, that, unfortunately, he never got to experience.

There are problems that should be eradicated from the world with the utmost urgency, such as three cases of trafficking that are terrible for mankind, drugs, weapons and prostitution, besides hunger and poverty, obviously. Child labour is, undoubtedly, another one.

Considering that economic power rules the world, the politicians unflinchingly obey to this oligarchy that hinders a world of liberty and peace impossible.

The motivation for many drug and alcohol rehabilitation clinics is the profit obtained with recovering addicts. The Portuguese government does very little to fight against this calamity, with methadone treatments and endless programs, but very few psychological monitoring. It is expensive for the State to support professionals that achieve good results. It is preferable to let them fall into criminality and prison, which is cheaper. Inevitably, more money will be spent with HIV medicines. Everyone is burying the head in sand. Prevention should start in Primary school and continue along the years.

Ricardo had crossed through a turbulent period of the Portuguese society. He had never had information about drugs, nor many others like him. It was like discovering the unknown, oblivious to the consequences that could come.

When he was brought to his knees, he had many wounds associated. All he had remaining was the support of his family to return to a normal life, free from drugs. Nine months of abstinence were not enough to solve the problems related to this awful curse on humanity.

Le Patriarche was a concept with good intentions, in essence. Over the years it took a different direction. It is believed that the association helped many young men and women. There are those who can only praise its supervisors and leaders. Ricardo, however, cannot say the same due to his psychological profile. By the end of his permanence in the association, he was completely disconnected from the community, said to be therapeutic.

Le Patriarche was, actually, a world apart, with its own laws and rules. It cannot be said that was subjected to the legislation of the countries where the centres were established. Some rituals were completely unacceptable, like throwing animal droppings over the heads of fresh newly-weds. This was utterly obscene and humiliating. When Ricardo witnessed this unpleasant and strange event, he could not believe it was true. That might show the social degradation and lack of affection from the part of the supervisors, who, in most cases, had no training to lead these groups. Seniority prevailed in the association. It was not common to see joy in the faces of the residents. Initially, many of them were depressed and *"davam-lhe na cabeça"*, a Portuguese expression, also used in the association that means to be brainwashed. The majority of the supervisors were rude men, without psychological preparation to carry out their role.

Before recounting the arrival of Ricardo at Portugal and the reunion with his family, there are some details during his stay in several centres that were somehow ludicrous. I am going to proceed narrating these.

The centre of the association was located thirteen miles from Narbonne. This is where Ricardo set foot for the first time in a communal addictions rehabilitation centre. After three weeks, he met Paula's mother, who was visiting her. The clothes were washed in a big tank of cold water. He felt a little constrained about washing his underwear. Surprisingly, Paula's mother offered to do it for him. She said that, certainly, he was not used to do it by himself. She was a very nice lady who managed to see that Ricardo was completely out of place. Even Paula, who had some affection for him, was surprised. Ricardo never forgot that situation all along his life. In that woman, he sees an example of service to your neighbour without hidden motives. She was truly a simple woman, who had suffered too much with the drug addiction of her daughter that seemed to be rehabilitated, fortunately. Ricardo gave her heartfelt thanks, certain that he would not see her and her daughter Paula again. He never ever saw anyone from the hundreds of persons he had met at the rehabilitation centres, again. Each of them left a part of themselves in his life, as he also left his mark in others, in a certain way.

While in route to Ireland, passing through Paris, they stopped for a few hours, to allow some rest from the long journey from the south of France. He had heard that Chartres was a big centre. Here, there were many more young girls, in their late teens. The movement of vehicles was enormous. Lorries were loaded and unloaded with materials and food supplies at all the time. When he was having the evening meal, he was assigned to store the washed cutlery. There might have been some two hundred persons dinning. A Portuguese woman was by his side doing the same task. She was amazed when she saw Ricardo drying the cutlery with a piece of cloth. Then, she told him: - "You'll never make it out of here doing it that way. Put the cutlery in the drawers still wet, tomorrow they'll be dry!"

Ricardo smiled to the young woman that seemed happy and answered: - "Maybe you're right! It's too much cutlery! Thanks for the tip."

Chartres might be the centre with the most advanced logistics, being the point of convergence of the association, in France. It looked like if nobody knew each other, such was the gathering of people waiting to be transferred to other centres. Lorries were constantly coming in and out. The canteens were completely crowded at meal times. By then, Ricardo was still lucid of his mind, only two months had passed since he had left Portugal. He was still under the effect of the medication although having stopped taking it. "The chemicals", they used to say, but forgetting that cigarettes were authorised, although obviously containing addictive chemicals.

All those rules imposed were rather complicated, making it hard to deal with at first. In the early months many escapes occurred, causing internal tensions. The presence of police authorities also threw the centres into turmoil. Everything could be worked out in a vertical way, with licensed health technicians, but the founder of the association was not quite worried about it. In the early days residents were authorised to drink wine. Later, it was strictly forbidden.

His first contact with Ireland was something new to Ricardo. The constant green of the landscape, the dark rocky hills glittering, made him feel a deep sense of liberty. However, that freedom was restricted to the car he was in. He could not leave, running free through the fields, feeling the freshness of the morning in his face and reach his young inner self, free from drugs.

It had been a paradoxical experience, with happy, but also anguishing moments. In the fields adjoining to the big house where they lived there were some pigs that, once, went on the loose. It was a rush, with everybody trying to catch them. Ricardo managed to ride one. He grabbed it by the ears, but the bloody pig was stronger and escaped despite his frustrated intent. Later, those pigs would be raised in pens and also fed by Ricardo, to serve as food for the residents. They did not kill them, of course. The pigs were sent to the slaughterhouse. After cleaned and butchered, the meat was stored in cooling chambers.

The worst part was not the leisure moments, but being enclosed, without any contact with other people and apart from civilization. They started to *"bater mal"*, a Portuguese expression that means to lose their mind. The fact of being twenty four hours a day with the same people, with very different characters, took its toll. Let us not forget that there were people from several countries, with different lifestyles and cultures. The Italians, who were offended by the others that were cutting the cooked spaghetti with the knife or the Mexican, who still acted like a member of a Los Angeles gang. John, a kid of Mexican origin had two brothers that had already been killed in gang fights, all because of settling of scores from drug trafficking.

The arrival of a team of "chantiers", residents specialised in building construction, from France, was the beginning of the end of Ricardo's adventure in Celtic lands. They came to reconstruct another small palace that belonged to the founder of the association. He carried on his back bags of one hundred and ten pounds of cement. He could not do anything else. He started to feel completely exhausted psychologically. His birthday was still celebrated in Cork. They made him a cake with candles, which Ricardo could not even blow out. The cake was cut by his colleagues, who together blew out the candles for him. The supervisor of the centre not even deigned to attend. He was in his office, together with other supervisors who had just arrived. When Ricardo, feebly, went to offer some of his birthday cake, they reproached his attitude. The following day, Ricardo left to France.

As stated before, Trouville looked more like a rest home for youths than a hospital of the association. It could be noticed that the residents had some economical possessions. They did not look as untidy as in the other centres. The chateau, where the terminally ill HIV patients resided, was probably from the late seventeenth century. It still retained all of its majesty and it was well preserved.

Ricardo believed that it would be there his last stay. There were rumours that he would be taken to Portugal, to another centre. Nevertheless, he wanted to go to his parents home, he missed them. The arrangements were being made. Then, one night, after Ricardo played the guitar beautifully, Carlos turned to him and calmly said: - "Ricardo, go and pack your bags. Tomorrow, we'll take you to the airport for you to go back home." Carlos always tried to watch over him day after day, making him to eat, unsuccessfully. Ricardo had stopped eating. He went on a hunger strike, oblivious to that. For three days he only had water.

Early morning, a Fiat Tempra was ready to drive off to Paris. Inside were Paulo, an Italian woman and, in the back, Ricardo was riding comfortably, like a lord.

When they arrived at Orly, Ricardo was handed over to the flight captain, who had already been instructed to receive him. Behind, remained the association Le Patriarche that Ricardo never visited again. In his mind he kept the memories of a period with highs and lows and many doubts.

He flew in executive class. The trip and all of its commodities were sponsored by his cousins, who were successful businessmen. The stewardesses were very kind. They knew that he was a sick person. Some Portuguese industrialists travelled next to him. They intended to be nice, making themselves available to help if he ever needed anything. Ricardo was still able to thank for their kindness.

The flight went on normally. The industrialists, who, in fact, were nouveau riche, were getting drunk with old whisky. They were constantly calling the stewardesses, but Ricardo was barely bothered.

After landing in Porto, escorted by the captain and a stewardess, he was taken to the arrivals area, where he was expected by his parents and some relatives.

Ricardo's father saw him in a glance and immediately ran to him. In an act of paternal love, he gave him a big hug. Ricardo, psychologically broken, was not even stirred, but his father could not contain the emotion of having his son back. His mother was smiling with contentment, as well as his uncle and aunt. The eyes of everyone were shining very brightly with joy.

Ricardo was told by his mother that he was going to Coimbra by ambulance and that she was accompanying him. He would need to stay in the psychiatric service as an inpatient. At least, his mother was going to try that he was accepted in the urgency services of the Hospital Universitário de Coimbra.

Lying on a stretcher in the urgencies, he could only hear, as in a hallucination, the doctors saying: - "Where is the man from outer space?" Meanwhile, a doctor arrived and examined him. She was not convinced that he needed to stay as an inpatient in the psychiatric ward. His mother was desperate and in tears. She was begging for the "alminhas", which means in a desperate way, that he was accepted or else he would go completely mad. Facing so much anguish, the doctor decided to question Ricardo a little further. This time she verified that there actually was some cognitive disorder. She was not a specialist in that field, so she called a colleague from Psychiatry, who, immediately, sent Ricardo to the psychiatric ward. He had been diagnosed with psychotic outbreaks, related to years of drug abuse.

The greatest flaw of Le Patriarche was that it failed absolutely in predicting that drug addiction might fuel mental disorders, such as chronic psychoses and even schizophrenia. This was the crucial point of divergence between the scientific community and the founder of the association. Even though he had no scientific knowledge or training in mental health, he wanted to make the world believe that everything could be solved with physical effort and herbal infusions. The pedagogy of the group meetings was merely washing dirty laundry in public. There were no consistent methodologies to make the new residents realise of the serious consequences of drug abuse.

The idea that many people makes of chemicals is questionable. Having an infection in any part of the body, they run to the doctor to take an antibiotic. But, what is an antibiotic, other than chemicals? And why cannot our brain deal with chemicals, if science also researched for years to treat mental illnesses? Let us not go into radicalism, for the end does not justify the means.

Ricardo would like to tell me that he had the most enriching experience in the association. However, his conscience does not allow it. According to him, in many years he never spoke about this with his friends. Now, the time had come to get it off his chest with me. We spent many long hours of conversation about this matter. Every time we have met, the subject was brought up. I had only heard wonders about the association until then. Nevertheless, articles published in the written press pointed out some criticism. This made me think of questioning an old friend of mine about my doubts.

Nowadays, Ricardo is a completely normal person. He takes the medicines that the so called experts of the association had denied him. Still, he means no harm to them. They helped many people that fact is for sure. Unfortunately, they were not successful with Ricardo. His parents always tried to do what was best for him, out of desperation to see him free from drugs and the lack of information at the time.

Maybe, in the future, Ricardo might try to meet the supervisors from his days at the association. Could they still be there? Or have they relapsed? Are they alive? He does not know. Life takes many twists and turns, and who knows, we might meet again in this crossroad that we live. No one knows but God!

It is a matter of necessity to bring back that the vast majority of the residents of the Association Le Patriarche were there to be free from drugs or alcohol. They were suffering souls, whose paths of life, caught in the web of drugs, had left deep scars, some hard too heal and others led even to a premature death. Each one had different life experiences to tell. Here lies another of the association's flaws. They had no one specialised to deal with each particular case of drug addiction. It should have been possible to debate in group meetings or individually with the technicians. This would have allowed a better understanding of their circumstances in regard to that calamity that ruined lives throughout the world with no distinction of social class.

The big issue of drug abuse is that its causes are defined by the personality of each individual. As we know, more than a disease, the consumption of drugs is an addiction that sets into people, frequently, at early ages. Society failed to prepare itself for a fight where the drug lords make colossal fortunes, set up companies for money laundering the proceeds of trafficking. The unfortunate ones are the drug abusers who are considered as marginal.

The illegality of this cursed business begins at the top. I believe that the legal drugs, also called social, are the first step into the illicit. When drank in excess, alcohol is tolerated by society, however, those who abuse it are marginalised.

Ricardo spent over a year without touching any alcohol, as it is, usually, a replacement for drugs. No matter how many treatments are done, there might be a relapse, sometimes fatal, if there is no strong will of body and soul to recover permanently.

Many of Ricardo's colleagues resorted to the association and each one had its own experience. Today, some of them are clean from drugs while others had already left to kingdom of heaven. Even though Ricardo was a moderate consumer, he acknowledged that any day could be his last. Still, his will to live prevailed. He even had a very short experience with the "intellectual" drug, cocaine. He thought seriously about the suffering that he was inflicting to his family. He decided it was time to put an end to his drug's cycle in a moment of Spiritual enlightenment. Nowadays, he has no problem whatsoever in talking about this matter. He tries to explain to the younger the entire process that leads to being addicted to this evil that destroys families and induces into crime, often violent. He told me over and over: -

"Presently, after all these years without drugs, I feel like a new man, with an infinite will to enjoy life."

Ricardo would like that the association had evolved to new concepts, namely in terms of the drugs liberation process. This fight is almost invariably unsuccessful. There are many vested interests in the business world. If the number of consumers reduces drastically, it will no longer be so profitable.

The money made with this business is staggering. It is related to weapons trafficking and extends to governments. Hence, a world free from drug trafficking will be always a world of peace and harmony between cultures. There is no doubt about it!

Ricardo had learnt that his past life had been his sole responsibility. He does not blame anyone for getting into drugs. He was given a head to think and he was aware of the damage he was inflicting to himself. As a result, he deals perfectly with his past and feels a great happiness for being free from that nightmare.

Once in a while, when we meet in a cafe, we have long conversations. He says that he does not understand how so many adult and mature people get caught into the web of drugs, with all the information available today. They did not have it when they were teenagers. According to him, these people should be approached in the streets, by specialised technicians, and referred for treatment, even if only ambulatory. This would be a way of lowering unemployment, generating jobs for skilled labour, like mental health or drug rehab technicians, whose jobs the State has the obligation to secure.

Ricardo believes that there is a key moment to abandon drugs. Then, a choice is presented to the drug addict; he has to decide whether he prefers life or a slow, painful death.

The drug abuser suffers from severe lack of affection. There are endless reasons for people to start using drugs and, consequently, get into violent crime. Marginalised people due to the fact of being from low classes, those who experienced an amorous disillusion, whatever!

It was far beyond Ricardo's comprehension how could governments refrain from pursuing an unrelenting fight against drug abuse. Some campaigns are launched just to appear in the media, as for the rest... When will the society mobilise? And take responsibility for the despair of thousands of families or for the agony of teenagers, suffering on the sidewalks after a night of alcohol and evil chemicals?

We were in complete consonance. It is not common that the media highlight news about drug addiction or alcohol abuse, including plans to fight or prevent them. The only articles seen in newspapers say: - "Man caught with drugs was arrested".

At the present, Ricardo does not want to know anything about drugs or Le Patriarche. They are reminiscences of a far gone past. Surely, he was not the only one; there are others who, like him, had gone through the same. It hurts him to the soul to see people consuming drugs when he passes by certain places that he cannot avoid. He goes through quietly, intending not to marginalise them. He had been through it and knows what is like to be in that nightmare.

"There are moments we experience in life when a light guides us to be free from evils that were originated in ourselves. Then, it takes insight to avoid losing that shining light that might illuminate us for the rest of our lives." Ricardo told me in one of the few talks we had lately.

It must be welcomed his will to live life without drugs. His eyes glittered like never before, despite his mental disorder, now completely under control, thanks to his medication. He leads an entirely normal life.

Currently, he has other distresses, just like any other ordinary citizen. They are unavoidable, although these issues do not depend on him, being the result of an unfair society, ruled by individuals obsessed with power and economic interests. Had we a more humane society, perhaps many of the problems with drug addictions would be residual. Thus, mankind would be happy and not subdued with extraneous problems.

Over twenty years had passed since Ricardo's days at Le Patriarche. Yet, once in a while, he still feels for those girls who had meals close to him in the big "Châteaux" at Trouville. He cannot forget their suffering caused by HIV in terminal phase, even if he wanted to. He will keep them forever in his memory. At least, he felt better in knowing that, until the end of their lives, certainly not too far, they would be comfortable and well cared.

Ricardo believes that Le Patriarche was nothing but a hoax. A pseudo-treatment community where some lived in the lap of luxury, while others, the transgressors of society, worked days in a row, for the elite, holder of the real estate assets of the founder. On behalf of Ricardo, I will not mention his name. He never saw him. It was like if he was invisible, enthroned by his disciples.

The name of the association said it all. Le Patriarche or **The Patriarch**, as if it meant: -"I am your father! Men and women marginalised by society, come to me... I will heal you from that addiction."

This experience through the association was due to a misinformed social assistant. By that time, it was in vogue. All individuals suffering from drug addiction were sent there. Ricardo told me, many years later, that the social workers from the social security should get right into the thick of things. They ought to leave their air conditioned offices and verify what was really going on in these centres. A friend of Ricardo was at death's door in another institution. He was saved from certain death, thanks to the Hospital of Coimbra. People in a state of fragility should not be sent to these institutions without knowing if they have the means to keep them safe, both psychologically and physically. We are not all the same and each individual is a particular case.

There are those who can only praise Le Patriarche today and it is their right. For some, maybe a few, it was a solution. But hundreds had to escape from the association. They were unable or had not been prepared to withstand the harsh methods in their daily activities.

Ricardo still recalls today, so many years after the events, that his period in the association was one of the most significant in his life and he still carries the best of it with him. It is sad that the members of the European Union do not regard this problem as a serious issue for society. Instead of arresting consumers and small-time drug traffickers, it would be better if therapeutic communities were set up at state level, with specialised technicians and not mere instructors or former drug addicts, many of them still on the verge of a relapse. Obviously, this is a large scale investment, but considering the payback to society in terms of reducing drug-related criminality, it is easily justifiable. Presently, those making money with the situation are the private clinics that charge an arm and a leg for a treatment program with one year's duration. On top of that, they promote themselves in the media, showing their projects as success stories, although they cost the earth, when youths could have free access to these treatments.

Ricardo remembers of a psychiatrist, well renowned in Portugal, that makes convincing speeches on the radio and television about matters such as sexology and drug addictions. However, in his private clinic he would not let a patient complete his treatment program due to his inability to pay the exorbitant monthly payment that was charged. Nevertheless, that same young man revealed a great character and personality. After just three months in the program, he left the clinic and remained clean from drugs for the rest of his life. A few years later, he wrote a letter asking to visit the rehabilitation centre. The famous psychiatrist, a cold and calculating individual, replied that it was not possible because he had not completed the treatment program. This example clearly shows to these so called experts that each individual has its own personality and should be treated accordingly. In addition, generalisation should be averted. It is important that mental health technicians are devoted to their patients and to the human cause. Tomorrow is always uncertain. Today we are under the spotlight and the next day we can be in the gutter, living on the breadline.

The State has the obligation to treat these individuals not as criminals but with dignity, as people suffering from an illness. Institutions like Le Patriarche should review their therapeutic methods, if they can be considered as such.

Looking back, Ricardo realises the time he wasted in the emptiness of drugs. Nowadays, as a mature man, he understands that the way he chose to live in the eighties meant that there was no escape from the rampant spreading of drugs. It is said that the Portuguese poet Fernando Pessoa, like other intellectuals, consumed drugs. That, however, was among the Portuguese elite, even though they were spiritual men, like many other artists. On the other hand, this is about ordinary people, the generality of a youth that are getting lost in the webs of this demonic addiction.

These days, Ricardo discovered many little pleasures far greater than the ones he experienced with drugs. He can think clearly and coherently, living as happily as he is allowed by himself and the society.

I like to meet with him, always serene and with a smile in his face when he sees me arriving. I feel his inner peace. The demons of addiction are far gone. Despite he had made his family suffer, the main suffering was brought onto him. It was a relentless fight. He had been through moments that he wishes to forget forever. He threw that black stone into a bottomless pit, so he would never see it again. Thus, he solved a serious problem that had been tormenting his life.

Le Patriarche was recorded on his mind as a dark passage of his life that, as time went by, faded into a clear path. In his newly found psychological freedom, the skies regained their celestial blue. His mind and body recovered completely, never giving signs of weakness again. His inner self has returned to its essence, proving wrong the "elders of Restelo"[1] and showing that recovery is possible, even in the most adverse situation.

In the House of Le Patriarche began the path that led him to the freedom of thinking and acting like any other human being.

THE END

---

[1] This portuguese expression is related to the epic poem "The Lusiads", written by portuguese 16th century poet Luís de Camões. In the episode of the Old Man of Restelo, in Canto IV, strophe 129, this figure symbolises the incredulity of Portuguese people about the voyages of discovery.

EPILOGUE

More than two decades had passed, when Ricardo visited the centre in Trouville, where he spent his last days at the association and almost came close to madness.

What once had been a luxury hospital complex was now completely abandoned and vandalised. This decay was like a mirror of the tragic ending of the association's founder. The gardens that used to be well-kept, with the trees perfectly pruned and the lawns cut regularly, were subjugated by the proliferating undergrowth that obstructed the passage. The doors and windows had been broken, except for the few that were still boarded.

Ricardo felt his skin crawl as he entered through the smashed main door of the impressive "Châteaux" of Trouville. The half-light allowed him to see the state of destruction of the building. The beautiful staircases in African Blackwood were rotting. The utter emptiness of the rooms was frightening, with plants creeping up through every opening. Along the walls graffiti and inscriptions could be seen, some with satanic allusions. Just by the entrance, a sentence was written in French: *"Si vous osez entrer dans ce bâtiment, vous ne pourrez jamais le quitter"*. Ricardo could deeply relate to it, as he had felt it so many times during his permanence, *"If you dare to enter this building, you can never leave"*. He shivered terribly and left in a hurry to the outside, where freedom and a healthy life expected him.

That return to the past was just an instant that he needed, in order to forget what could not be ever forgotten.

www.ingramcontent.com/pod-product-compliance
Lightning Source LLC
Chambersburg PA
CBHW030520290526
45786CB00004B/1548